THE BATTLE OF THE MIND

THE JOURNEY TO FREEDOM AND VICTORY

BRENDALEE BONNIE

THE BATTLE OF THE MIND. Copyright @ 2025. Brendalee Bonnie. All rights reserved.

No part of this publication may be reproduced, stored in a retrieval system or transmitted in any form or by any means, electronic, mechanical, photocopying, recording or otherwise without the prior written permission of the author.

Published by:

Editor: Cleveland O. McLeish (Author C. Orville McLeish)

ISBN: 978-1-965635-23-0 (paperback)

Scripture quotations marked "NKJV" are taken from the New King James Version. Copyright © 1982 by Thomas Nelson, Inc. Used by permission. All rights reserved. Bible text from the New King James Version® is not to be reproduced in copies or otherwise by any means except as permitted in writing by Thomas Nelson, Inc., Attn: Bible Rights and Permissions, P.O. Box 141000, Nashville, TN 37214-1000.

TABLE OF CONTENTS

Introduction 5

Chapter 1: Mindset Matters 9

Chapter 2: Resetting the Mind 33

Chapter 3: The Mindset of a Warrior 51

The Prayer of Deliverance and Freedom 69

My Notes 71

The Journey to Destiny Series 73

Aspiring to Inspire 75

INTRODUCTION

A question was asked of me as I expressed my feelings of being overwhelmed and feeling that I have come to the end of this journey with a trusted friend. I felt extremely frustrated, confused, defused, oppressed, distressed, and absolutely hopeless. I kept repeating the words of defeat, ***"Life does not make any sense."*** She quietly listened, and after a long pause, she asked this very important question as was led, ***"What is the battle over? Your mind, emotion, or call?"***

This question, as released, stopped me in my tracks and brought me back to immediate spiritual consciousness—to the point where I immediately recognized and admitted that this was an outright war on all three, but the core was the mind.

This sudden response and the depth of the question connected immediately with my spirit and subconsciousness. I immediately realized that there was a battle going on. It was not just my feeling, nor was this experience natural, but it was absolutely spiritual. There was a war going on in the spirit for territory, that of my mind. My emotions were targeted, so I was distracted from focusing on what I knew I was called to do.

Even though I was echoing the feeling of defeat because what I was experiencing was extremely overwhelming, deep down within, I knew I was never defeated.

The Battle of the Mind

This question immediately pulled me together gradually, and the reality, fact, and truth began unfolding. I began to change my perspective and perception of the matter at hand.

As I began responding, the answers just came to me. It all lay within but was hidden because I was distracted by my feelings/emotions and, as such, was disconnected in my spirit from what was really happening: the battle engaged and enraged in my mind, which was triggering the signs and symptoms being experienced not just mentally but physically because there was tension in my head and entire body.

The symptoms were extremely overbearing, and I felt so alone in it. Everything was saying, "Just quit because this is it," but, like in the story of Elijah where God showed up, and in the story of David where Jonathan showed up, the angel in the form of this friend showed up just when I was at my wit's end. Men are doors, and doors are men. We are someone's angel; we are someone's Jonathan; we are God's eyes, ears, mouth, hands, and feet extended to others in their times of need.

The ears and mouth of the learned was activated at that minute and she was able to speak a word in season because she sensed the reason.

Thank God for accountability partners that are God-given or God-sent. It is important to have that confidant, accountability partner, the right connection/association as seen in Ecclesiastes 4:9-10, *"Two are better than one, because they have a good reward for their labor. For if they fall, one will lift up his companion. But woe to him who is alone when he falls, for he has no one to help him up." (NKJV).*

The Battle of the Mind

The battle of the mind is real, just as the battle for your life is, because where the mind goes, your life flows. Truth is, many depend on your success and victory. In other words, you winning this battle is critical to others whose life depends on your victory. If you die in this battle, others depending on you will never live to come out alive either. You are to be delivered to be a deliverer. You are to be victorious to make others also experience victory in what seems to be their pit of defeat or their disastrous destiny in life. Many will benefit from your battles and victories when you have won, so don't retreat and concede defeat.

Following the attack, I was challenged to release this book as I heard in my spirit, *"The area of attack is where you will have your greatest comeback, and you are delivered to be a deliverer to others in a similar situation or war/battle."*

CHAPTER 1

MINDSET MATTERS

Mindset matters because, according to Romans 7:25, it is with the mind that man serves his Creator, the one true and living God. As such, the enemy seeks to launch his attack and try to mess with this engine that causes man to function according to God's design and purposes.

The mind also serves as the spiritual womb of mankind. What do the mind and the womb have in common? The mind is the womb of your life where word seeds are planted or sown, trees are grown, and fruit is produced. These words collectively are known as thoughts. They can either be of a positive or negative nature. Its nature determines the effect and results experienced and given.

Like the womb, where conception occurs, and the fetus is nurtured and carried to full term for birthing, our mind operates accordingly. As such, we must be extremely careful and vigilant regarding the kind of seed deposited in the womb of our life: the mind.

The greatest wealth is salvation; next in line is the goal to possess and maintain a healthy body and mind. As such, an overactive or super busy mind is also one that is in the danger zone. Overthinking

The Battle of the Mind

is unhealthy, whether the thoughts are healthy or unhealthy. We are guided to think right thoughts, but everything can be bad even when it is good because it is over-exhausted.

The enemy thrives and capitalizes on every opportunity presented to him through overindulging minds. He can use whatever was intended for good to his disadvantage if we refuse to be wise.

Be careful that the mind doesn't become congested. Even the best of thoughts, if not managed properly, can be to our disadvantage, especially when the mind becomes super busy, overcrowded, or overpopulated with thoughts. The enemy can and will use an over-processed or super busy mind to his disadvantage and to your demise, so be wise in managing the thought processes of your mind.

The war or battle of the mind begins when the wrong words are being sown and developed within it. There is continual contention for dominion over the mind as the enemy seeks to intercept and hijack it with the wrong words or thoughts. We must contend with the determination to triumph, conquer, and ultimately win this battle.

The battle is waged there because that is where the seed of purpose and destiny is conceived, developed, incubated, nurtured, and birthed.

The enemy attacks the mind with the intention of aborting God's destiny and purpose by sowing seeds of doubt and fear, causing barrenness, hopelessness, and despair, with the intention of giving birth to his purpose and fulfilling his evil agenda. *How, why could, or should all this be happening? How and when will this be? Where and when will this come to an end? Could this be what is happening*

The Battle of the Mind

and how it will end? According to one's perception and perspective of things, the questions fuel these floods of reasoning, pondering, wondering, and wandering. All this is triggered by the presence of a genuine situation, which is evidence of worry, anxiety, fear, uncertainty, and insecurity. With a mind extremely bombarded and emotions unstable, head feeling like it is about to explode, and heart pounding as if someone is pursuing you, you feel as if this is the end; there is no strength to resist what is happening as the feeling becomes more and more overwhelming. *With anxiety level rising and seemingly exceeding the limit like a car that is about to crash, how do I regain control?* It seems oh so impossible, and you are being told internally that this has no stopping or means of gaining control—that it is the enemy—that troll—speaking lies into your soul as he tries to take control, seeking to bring you to mental wreckage. You try hard to resist the racing thoughts and the pounding heart that makes your entire body nervous and shake as if you are about to physically fall apart, and it seems so hard. All this becomes so overbearing, and you begin thinking, *"How do I put an end to all this?"*

Yes, I understand quite well what you are experiencing because I too have been at that place. Trying as hard as I may, but this would not stop: this bombardment of tormenting and torturing thoughts following one after the other, not even a space to breathe. *Will it ever end? How did I get here, and how do I get out of here?* Yes, being at that place where life seems like it makes no sense and there is no positive meaning to living.

Yes, it all began in the mind: reasonings, wonderings, ponderings, rationalizing, waverings; feelings of insecurity and uncertainty, a multitude of thoughts flowing in and out and causing traffic obstruction and combustion. There was no time for my mind to

The Battle of the Mind

breathe because the space was over-occupied with negative and unhealthy thoughts. Yes, this was a bomb rush that gave me no time to breathe. I was now far off mentally and emotionally, wandering in a wilderness of weeds of negativity. I saw and thought only the opposite of what God would have said. It all began with one wrong seed or thought of negativity sown in my head. These are the seeds the enemy begins with—one nagging thought which, when incubated, brings offspring of many others.

They seem at first to be so insignificant and non-impactful, but subtly, they are negatively impacting your emotions, disturbing, interrupting, and subtracting your peace and adding to your life's torment and misery.

You begin to wonder, ponder, rationalize, and reason until you have wandered and roamed to a dark place of seemingly no return. You are now farther than you had fathomed that you would have gone. Yes, this is where it all began.

It was so subtle and seemingly innocent, so much so that you did not make much of it. Before you realize or know it, you have given the devil a foothold in your mind, and he has maximized on this and trespassed and erected his stronghold. You begin to incubate and nurture and eventually begin to give birth to it as, emotionally, mentally, and physically, you begin to be negatively impacted by it. You gave the enemy a yard, and he took the whole mile and extended it to miles and miles, stealing even your joy/peace/smile. You gave him the finger, and he took the whole hand and began to wave his evil wand in your mind. Before you know it, you find yourself at that place where you begin to wonder how you got there and how you can get out of there. It seems like the point of no return; so hopeless.

The Battle of the Mind

Have you ever been to a place where your life seems like it doesn't make sense anymore? It began with just one thing that does not seem to be going as right as you thought it would. It then gave you feelings of disappointment and discouragement, as if you were denied and betrayed. I too was at that place and, as such, understand exactly how you felt or are feeling.

Whenever you are at this point, I suggest you pause and be still for a while until you are able to think clearly. Begin to reflect on your life and God's goodness extended accordingly. Consider just being alive at that very minute and see it as the biggest blessing or gift you could ever possess and are possessing. Recognize the lies that Satan is whispering in your ears. Acknowledge and identify that every wrong thought that causes you to be at that place is a lie being whispered in your ear, an evil seed being planted in your mind, and an unhealthy energy being fed into your spirit.

You must acknowledge and understand that even though it may look and feel like it, that doesn't mean that it is it. Fear is false evidence appearing to be real. You receive and will be or become like any package you have signed for. If you sign for victory, this will be your portion; likewise, if you sign for defeat, then that will be your portion or manifestation. As such, never let your feelings vote and determine the outcome of your destiny. Your life should be lived by God's design and not by crisis or your circumstances. You should walk by faith and not by fear of what you are feeling or seeing.

There is too much to gain to lose by surrendering control of your mind to the enemy. It is not God's will for the enemy to succeed or triumph in this battle over your mind, even though it may be divinely permitted as a result of your violation of God's

The Battle of the Mind

commandment or plan. Despite this, you are still in His hand, and as such, He will not permit your foot to be moved or be put to shame.

Yes, it all begins in the mind, and that is why the mind matters. The war of words are arrows, javelins, spears, and swords intended to enter your soul and spirit, mess with your emotion and mental faculty, and take you off course via distraction. Contend by guarding your mind: what you hear and see and perceive of it, because it begins with a little nagging seed called thought, which begins to grow in reasoning, and your mind then goes wandering so far that you begin to feel frustrated, confused, discouraged, disappointed, drained and defeated.

Guard your heart and mind against what you hear and see; do this intentionally, diligently, and consistently. This is how you contend because the opposition's mission is to distract you, so you will lose your focus, drain your energy, and steal your peace, joy, and happiness. The enemy doesn't have the luxury of peace of mind and joy divine, so he seeks to rob this from anyone who possesses or seeks to have it.

> *For I know the thoughts that I think toward you, says the LORD, thoughts of peace and not of evil, to give you a future and a hope. (Jeremiah 29:11 – NKJV).*

> *The thief does not come except to steal, and to kill, and to destroy. I have come that they may have life, and that they may have it more abundantly. (John 10:10 – NKJV).*

Each attack is strategic and is intended to catch you off guard and take you off track, just when you are experiencing those precious moments of peace and joy. He tries to cause a setback after each comeback. You are being watched or monitored; yes, you are under evil surveillance, but the all-seeing and unseen eyes and caring hands carefully watch over and guard and protect you as you abide in Him and keep your mind on Him.

> *You will keep him in perfect peace, whose mind is stayed on You, because he trusts in You. (Isaiah 26:3 – NKJV).*

Be vigilant and sober and be aware of the enemy's strategy, device, and timing.

> *Be sober, be vigilant; because your adversary the devil walks about like a roaring lion, seeking whom he may devour. (1 Peter 5:8 – NKJV).*

> *Lest Satan should take advantage of us; for we are not ignorant of his devices. (2 Corinthians 2:11 – NKJV).*

Never quit because of what you are experiencing. Never quit because it seems confusing and seems to be making no sense. Never quit on yourself, on God or your purpose and destiny because it seems like nothing positive seems to be forthcoming or the promise does not seem to be fulfilling. God has a set timing, and as such, the waiting period is extremely important. At this critical stage of your life, protect your head by guarding your mind because if garbage is dumped there, it will begin to flow from it. Do not allow the devil to use your mind as his dumpster. Manage your mind wisely and you will manage your life and protect and preserve your destiny found in Christ.

The Battle of the Mind

Master or be mastered, conquer or be conquered, defeat or be defeated, overcome or be overcome. What will it be, victory or defeat?

Never quit in the battle of the mind. Keep holding on to what God says concerning you. Believe that He will perfect that which concerns you and Him, and as such, will work all things out together for your good and His glory.

This was the mindset David had. He exhibited his confident trust in His God's goodness and faithfulness towards him, even in the face of adversity. This he penned in Psalm 138:8.

> *The LORD will perfect that which concerns me; Your mercy, LORD, endures forever; Do not forsake the works of Your hands. (Psalm 138:8 – NKJV).*

David understood the importance of having the right mindset as a mighty warrior. He understood that the outcome of his life and the purpose to which he was called depended on him cultivating the right mind. As such, mindset mattered to his prosperity and success as King of Israel and securing victory for the nation, people, and the God he represented.

We see where, as needed and as much as he could, he sought to encourage himself when the battle or war of the mind ensued; yes, in his adversities, he took courage and strength in God and maintained a right mind and spirit. He encouraged himself as he sang and penned his Psalms of praises and prayers of petitions, thanksgiving, and assurances of his confident trust in God. By doing this, he was guarding his mind against doubt and fear according to any and every contradicting reality he faced. We see where, despite the many challenges, David saw God for who He was in his current situations: Rock, Fortress, Refuge, Hiding Place, Shepherd, Keeper, Light, Salvation, Dwelling Place, Deliverer, Shield, Healer, Saviour, Peace, Joy, Strength, Provider, etc. In your situation, God can be who He is supposed to be if you, like David, acknowledge Him for who He is and you want Him to manifest as accordingly, at that time of need. It all begins with the mindset that you cultivate and maintain.

Likewise, Paul demonstrated in 2 Corinthians 11:23-28 and Romans 8:28–39 that he too was confident that even with being frequently imprisoned, and with all the 39 stripes received from being beaten several times with rods, stoned, suffering shipwreck on three occasions, experienced rejection by his own brethren, among many other persecutions and afflictions, even abandonment by spiritual brethren, he would allow none of this or nothing else to cause him to be separated from his relationship with God. He would not allow this to take his heart from God or change his mind toward Him. He saw these as advantages and not disadvantages concerning him. He saw that despite all these, he was more than a conqueror and was victorious because they all worked for and not against him and helped him successfully fulfil God's purpose for his life to its fullest.

If the children of Israel, who died in the wilderness and did not transition to the Promised Land, had this mindset, the outcome would have been different. Instead, they could only see the negative and magnified their current circumstances and made equal confessions to which they later succumbed, as seen in Numbers 14:26-35.

The Battle of the Mind

> *And the LORD spoke to Moses and Aaron, saying, "How long shall I bear with this evil congregation who complain against Me? I have heard the complaints which the children of Israel make against Me. Say to them, 'As I live,' says the LORD, 'just as you have spoken in My hearing, so I will do to you: The carcasses of you who have complained against Me shall fall in this wilderness, all of you who were numbered, according to your entire number, from twenty years old and above. Except for Caleb the son of Jephunneh and Joshua the son of Nun, you shall by no means enter the land which I swore I would make you dwell in. But your little ones, whom you said would be victims, I will bring in, and they shall know the land which you have despised. But as for you, your carcasses shall fall in this wilderness. And your sons shall be shepherds in the wilderness forty years, and bear the brunt of your infidelity, until your carcasses are consumed in the wilderness. According to the number of the days in which you spied out the land, forty days, for each day you shall bear your guilt one year, namely forty years, and you shall know My rejection. I the LORD have spoken this. I will surely do so to all this evil congregation who are gathered together against Me. In this wilderness they shall be consumed, and there they shall die.'" (Numbers 14:26-35 – NKJV).*

According to Hebrews 3:16-19, and as seen in Numbers 26:64-65, unbelief grieves God. He is allergic to murmuring, grumbling, complaining, and doublemindedness. He is not pleased with ungratefulness. This was the wilderness mindset that cost the wilderness wanderers and wonderers dearly; it cost them their lives and robbed them of their prophetic destiny. They were delivered but did not and could not maintain their deliverance and freedom and

The Battle of the Mind

were hindered from entering, conquering, accessing, and possessing because of their negative mental attitude or mindset.

We see where Joshua and Caleb, with a different mindset—one of a positive mental attitude—received the mega or huge; they lived to see the goodness of the Lord in the land of the living. Even at age eighty-five, Caleb was adamant that he was to be given his inheritance because even then, he was well able to conquer and possess that which God had promised him. He was not going to be limited or restricted by age—he would have none of it.

> *Then the children of Judah came to Joshua in Gilgal. And Caleb the son of Jephunneh the Kenizzite said to him: "You know the word which the LORD said to Moses the man of God concerning you and me in Kadesh Barnea. I was forty years old when Moses the servant of the LORD sent me from Kadesh Barnea to spy out the land, and I brought back word to him as it was in my heart. Nevertheless my brethren who went up with me made the heart of the people melt, but I wholly followed the LORD my God. So Moses swore on that day, saying, 'Surely the land where your foot has trodden shall be your inheritance and your children's forever, because you have wholly followed the LORD my God.' And now, behold, the LORD has kept me alive, as He said, these forty-five years, ever since the LORD spoke this word to Moses while Israel wandered in the wilderness; and now, here I am this day, eighty-five years old. As yet I am as strong this day as on the day that Moses sent me; just as my strength was then, so now is my strength for war, both for going out and for coming in. Now therefore, give me this mountain of which the LORD spoke in that day; for you heard in that day how the Anakim were there, and that the*

The Battle of the Mind

> *cities were great and fortified. It may be that the LORD will be with me, and I shall be able to drive them out as the LORD said." And Joshua blessed him, and gave Hebron to Caleb the son of Jephunneh as an inheritance. (Joshua 14:6-13 – NKJV).*

When our mindset is negative, our report will be derogative, degrading, and discouraging; when our mindset is positive, our report will be uplifting, encouraging, and life-giving.

> *Then they came to the Valley of Eshcol, and there cut down a branch with one cluster of grapes; they carried it between two of them on a pole. They also brought some of the pomegranates and figs. The place was called the Valley of Eshcol, because of the cluster which the men of Israel cut down there. And they returned from spying out the land after forty days. Now they departed and came back to Moses and Aaron and all the congregation of the children of Israel in the Wilderness of Paran, at Kadesh; they brought back word to them and to all the congregation, and showed them the fruit of the land. Then they told him, and said: "We went to the land where you sent us. It truly flows with milk and honey, and this is its fruit. Nevertheless the people who dwell in the land are strong; the cities are fortified and very large; moreover we saw the descendants of Anak there. The Amalekites dwell in the land of the South; the Hittites, the Jebusites, and the Amorites dwell in the mountains; and the Canaanites dwell by the sea and along the banks of the Jordan." Then Caleb quieted the people before Moses, and said, "Let us go up at once and take possession, for we are well able to overcome it." But the men who had gone up with him said, "We are not able to go up against the people, for*

The Battle of the Mind

> *they are stronger than we." And they gave the children of Israel a bad report of the land which they had spied out, saying, "The land through which we have gone as spies is a land that devours its inhabitants, and all the people whom we saw in it are men of great stature. There we saw the giants (the descendants of Anak came from the giants); and we were like grasshoppers in our own sight, and so we were in their sight." (Numbers 13:23-33 – NKJV).*

Paul won the war by doing this one thing: forgetting the things that are behind and pressing toward the higher calling. Look beyond your past failures and mistakes and press forward towards a new beginning and fresh start, as seen in Isaiah 43:18-19.

Paul maintained the right mindset and, as such, even in prison—being physically incarcerated—he was spiritually free and emancipated as he fed his mind on the Word and could feed others even from that place of his current state and encourage their faith accordingly.

I too had to fight to put my past behind me and focus forward to overcome and win the battle over the mind. I lived on medications, and the doctor's office was once my place of refuge, but God gave me a word from 2 Timothy 1:7 in the wee hours of one particular night when the spirit of fear and anxiety visited as usual. This scripture and many other similar references became my point of reference. Prayer and declaration, according to the scripture and their respective references given, were used as my shield, sword, defense, and deliverance. From my personal experience and encounter came my personal and famous quotes, **"My meditation is my medication"** and **" I was born to win, and I live to conquer."**

The Battle of the Mind

The children of Israel needed a mind reset because they were contaminated concerning their beliefs and heritage as a result of the association with the mixed multitude. As such, they could only see themselves as a victim of their current situation.

A victim mindset results from the venom of the sting of negativity from the serpent/adversary. The only antidote is the constant application of faith injection of the Word of God for the respective situation. Through its constant application, you will eventually emerge and see yourself for who you were designed to be: forever the victor, never the victim. During the battle, whatever you concede to, you will become: defeat or victory, victor or victim.

What do you do when the reality of the wilderness hits you? Do you think defeat, speaking like a victim, and seeing only your current reality? Do you murmur and complain instead of remembering, standing on, and declaring what God said concerning you?

When you declare what you have heard God say, you are guarding and protecting your head from the dart and arrow of negative and contradicting thoughts hurled at your mind by the enemy.

There are so many times when I have found myself at the seemingly place of defeat, and the circumstances of defeat feel so real. At this time, when the reality of my feelings becomes overwhelming, I immediately make this audible verbal confession to God and in the ear of the adversary, *"God, I am feeling defeated; however, even though I am feeling defeated, I know that I am never defeated. I always win because You always cause me to triumph and nothing is working against me, but all things are working for my good and for Your glory."* I kid you not; at this point, I feel deliverance, freedom, strength, triumph, and the motivation to go on. I begin to

The Battle of the Mind

feel like a victor, an overcomer, conqueror, and a winner. I then know that, once again, Satan was defeated because he thought he had me. He stood by, waiting to see me fall; instead, he saw my faith rise right before his eyes. The table of victory was spread right before his eyes, and the transaction was reversed; the table turned, and the script flipped.

As the Word of God rightly states in Proverbs 18:21, *"Death and life are in the power of the tongue; and those who love it will eat its fruit." (NKJV).*

Be encouraged that whatever battle you go through, you are expected to win so you can teach someone going through a similar situation how to triumph. The war is not about you but who you are called to be and what you are called to do. The war is an attempt to discredit the power and potency of God and His kingdom here on earth. Also, the battle of the mind is to limit you so God can be restricted or limited to freely operate in and through your life for your good and His glory.

As we look at the story of the centurion in Matthew 8:5-13, there was no reasoning, wondering, or second-guessing what God, through Jesus Christ, was capable of doing. He knew that with God, as seen in Luke 1:37, all things are possible: nothing is or will ever be impossible. Every Red Sea and River Jordan is passable or crossable, every Jericho Wall is destructible, every mountain is moveable, and every barren womb is conceivable.

The right mindset reset leads to overall prosperity and success of the spirit, soul, and body, as seen in Romans 12:2, and as such, it is everything because through it comes the victory.

The Battle of the Mind

Whatever or all decisions arrived at begins and ends in the mind.

> *And do not be conformed to this world, but be transformed by the renewing of your mind, that you may prove what is that good and acceptable and perfect will of God. (Romans 12:2 – NKJV).*

To endure or persevere through trials, persecutions, adversities, and all the atrocities of life, we must cultivate and maintain the mindset of a warrior. We must be like-minded to that of Christ, who, for the sake of the joy of the prize set before His eyes, endured and persevered through pain in order to produce or fulfill His God-given purpose.

> *looking unto Jesus, the author and finisher of our faith, who for the joy that was set before Him endured the cross, despising the shame, and has sat down at the right hand of the throne of God. (Hebrews 12:2 – NKJV).*

He saw a greater glory or gain emerging from His pain or traumatic story.

> *For I consider that the sufferings of this present time are not worthy to be compared with the glory which shall be revealed in us. (Romans 8:18 – NKJV).*

It is said that purpose can be produced out of one's pain, and we see this to be evidently true throughout the life of Christ as He walked this earth. His rejection led to Him ministering to the rejected and freeing those captive souls of the bondage called rejection.

The Battle of the Mind

It had to come with the mindset of a warrior that required humility and numbness to this pain caused by rejection to overcome this obstacle or hurdle in order to keep running the race set before Him with and by faith.

Rejection was an everyday life experience for Jesus Christ, but because He had girded up the loins of His mind with truth, He was able to see the good in all of the bad He was experiencing. He saw the greater glory and impact that He was sent to the earth to create—to save and transform lives, heal the brokenhearted, set the captives free, and redirect the rejects to the life ordained for them and help them understand how loved and accepted they are in God's eye. He was sent to heal the wounds that rejection had made on many lives.

It was with the mindset of a warrior that Christ bore our grief, sorrow, and shame.

> *He is despised and rejected by men, A Man of sorrows and acquainted with grief. And we hid, as it were, our faces from Him; He was despised, and we did not esteem Him. Surely He has borne our griefs and carried our sorrows; Yet we esteemed Him stricken, smitten by God, and afflicted. But He was wounded for our transgressions, He was bruised for our iniquities; the chastisement for our peace was upon Him, and by His stripes we are healed. (Isaiah 53:3-5 – NKJV).*

Go forward with a mind girded and guarded with truth, as seen in 1 Peter 1:13, Philippians 4:8, John 8:32, and John 8:36.

The Battle of the Mind

> *Therefore gird up the loins of your mind, be sober, and rest your hope fully upon the grace that is to be brought to you at the revelation of Jesus Christ; (1 Peter 1:13 – NKJV).*

> *And you shall know the truth, and the truth shall make you free." (John 8:32 – NKJV).*

> *Therefore if the Son makes you free, you shall be free indeed. (John 8:36 – NKJV).*

> *Finally, brethren, whatever things are true, whatever things are noble, whatever things are just, whatever things are pure, whatever things are lovely, whatever things are of good report, if there is any virtue and if there is anything praiseworthy—meditate on these things. (Philippians 4:8 – NKJV).*

Cast down every thought that you acknowledge has intruded on your mind and is not of God.

> *casting down arguments and every high thing that exalts itself against the knowledge of God, bringing every thought into captivity to the obedience of Christ. (2 Corinthians 10:5 – NKJV).*

Maintain a mindset that doesn't settle for less than what Christ came, died, and rose for—the best, the eternal and abundant life, one of victory.

> *For God so loved the world that He gave His only begotten Son, that whoever believes in Him should not perish but have everlasting life. For God did not send His*

> *Son into the world to condemn the world, but that the world through Him might be saved. (John 3:16-17 – NKJV).*
>
> *This Book of the Law shall not depart from your mouth, but you shall meditate in it day and night, that you may observe to do according to all that is written in it. For then you will make your way prosperous, and then you will have good success. (Joshua 1:8 – NKJV).*

The mind matters; as such, it needs to be decluttered. That is where the war is and what the strife is over: the mind. It is a treasure and a prized possession envied by the enemy. It is with the mind that a man thinks, acts, and responds. It is the hub of operation or the processing center. Like the computer, it is your CPU [Central Processing Unit]. Here facts and truths are processed. Like it is often said, whatever goes in is what comes out as a byproduct. If garbage or lies get in, then the byproduct is the fruit or offspring thereof. When incubated, nurtured, and cultivated, whatever gets in as a seed brings forth fruit of its kind: a product of the mind. In other words, whatever is planted and if not uprooted will bring forth fruit eventually.

It is very important to think about what you are thinking and avoid too many racing thoughts vying for the attention of your heart/spirit. I would say unnecessary reasoning, pondering and wondering must be avoided because it will eventually result in your mind wandering. The mind has gone for a walk, straying so far from the path, and there is now a struggle to restrain it and return it to its rightful place.

The Battle of the Mind

The cares of the world can put a strain on the mind if we allow it to (see Matthew 6:25-34, Matthew 13:1-23). As such, boundaries are necessary for our mind to properly monitor our thought process.

> *Keep your heart with all diligence, for out of it spring the issues of life. (Proverbs 4:23 – NKJV).*

May the peace of God cover us, and may the peace of God take over our minds. He won't take over what we do not give Him control of or access to. It is only Satan who operates like that. He holds us against our will and forces, through his tool of oppression, to give in to him: his lies, deceit, and evil scheme. His only intent is to kill, steal, and destroy, as seen in John 10:10.

Here is a word of hope for you: Jesus Christ came to counteract this lie and evil plan, as seen in Colossians 2:15, "*Having disarmed principalities and powers, He made a public spectacle of them, triumphing over them in it.*" When He came, died, rose, and ascended, He destroyed every plan of the enemy. All we need to do is accept, receive, and appropriate this full and free salvation and walk in liberty mentally, emotionally, spiritually, and physically. This available package is comprehensive. It includes salvation, healing, and deliverance—saving your mind from the crime of unhealthy thinking. Access healing for your mind from serious wounds caused by evil, malicious, and destructive thoughts, and receive deliverance for your mind from unhealthy, unholy, and wrong thought-patterns.

You don't have to be forever trapped or engaged in that evil mind game. It is not one you want to play. Stay away from it. It is destructive, and that is why the devil has constructed it and seeks whomever he desires to be destroyed by it to become involved in

The Battle of the Mind

it—that evil mind game called the battle of the mind—for good or evil.

> *I find then a law, that evil is present with me, the one who wills to do good. (Romans 7:21 – NKJV).*
>
> *For the flesh lusts against the Spirit, and the Spirit against the flesh; and these are contrary to one another, so that you do not do the things that you wish. (Galatians 5:17 – NKJV).*

God gave us the power and strategy to overcome evil. Use it to conquer and overcome. Use the Word of God as your armory and use it effectively and fight this war over your mind with the objective to win it.

> *Finally, my brethren, be strong in the Lord and in the power of His might. Put on the whole armor of God, that you may be able to stand against the wiles of the devil. For we do not wrestle against flesh and blood, but against principalities, against powers, against the rulers of the darkness of this age, against spiritual hosts of wickedness in the heavenly places. Therefore take up the whole armor of God, that you may be able to withstand in the evil day, and having done all, to stand. Stand therefore, having girded your waist with truth, having put on the breastplate of righteousness, and having shod your feet with the preparation of the gospel of peace; above all, taking the shield of faith with which you will be able to quench all the fiery darts of the wicked one. And take the helmet of salvation, and the sword of the Spirit, which is the word of God; praying always with all prayer and supplication in the Spirit, being watchful to this end*

The Battle of the Mind

> *with all perseverance and supplication for all the saints— (Ephesians 6:10-18 - NKJV).*

The war of the mind is intended to shift your focus and have you disoriented or confused.

Whenever you find your mind going on a roller coaster ride, stop and get off immediately. The Holy Spirit did not take you there. The devil took you for that ride. It is not for free; you will eventually pay for it with the cost of your peace of mind. The enemy's intention is to thwart the purpose and prophetic destiny for your life in accordance with God's plan.

There can be a comeback from the setback caused by the war of the mind. It all begins with you individually taking responsibility over that which was entrusted to you, even before you were formed in your mother's womb: your mind (see Psalm 139:2-4,13). The key to your mind was given to you to lock and unlock, and you wisely choose who you give access to it.

The fight is real, the struggle is real, the battle is real, and the field is your mind, for which the enemy is seeking to gain ground. If he can get a foothold there, he can erect his stronghold there and make it his throne from which to rule and reign in your life. Resist giving your mind to the devil to execute his agenda. You must fight to evict, never allow yourself to get tricked into it, be fully equipped and well-armed with the Word of God, and keep fighting with the Sword of the Spirit. Lift your shield of faith, quench every fiery dart, and outsmart the enemy. Cover your head with the blood of Jesus, your helmet of salvation; being saved by grace through faith. Gird up your loins by filling your mind with truth and meditating

The Battle of the Mind

on God's Word day and night until it becomes a lamp to your feet and a light to your path and is continually stored in your heart.

As Joshua was challenged, let not the book of the Lord containing His laws depart from your mind/heart. Meditate on it continually and intentionally until your mind is conformed to His and your life transformed into His image and likeness, and you begin to look like Him in thoughts, words and deeds. Your mindset determines your reality. As such, it is important that you cultivate a positive, growth-oriented mindset, and you will find opportunities in every challenge or adversity.

We are never held back by people, places, things, or our circumstances. We are hindered from becoming the best version of ourselves because we refuse to shed the layers of comfort that hold us back. In order to go forward, we must embrace the discomfort of growth, and we will begin to discover and walk in our true potential.

Though the battle of the mind may seem general, it has varied aspects of it and is different in nature. For some, this battle targets your purpose and destiny concerning your spiritual life, family life, health, financial life, relationships, marriage life, children, job or business, and ministry.

Be kind to your mind by fighting to maintain a healthy one: guard it with due diligence.

CHAPTER 2

RESETTING THE MIND

Resetting the mind is the way to rewind and move forward on the right path and the path to long-lasting victory. We reset by renewing, restarting, and refocusing. Do this as often as you have to in order to get it right; do not mind it; just do not quit because it takes time for damage control, repair, and restoration to be done.

You are not alone on this journey of resetting the mind. Millions on the journey with you have either been this way, about to enter, or just exiting this path on the journey of the battle of the mind.

One of our biblical points of reference is a great man of God called Prophet Elijah. He had just, through God, won a major battle on Mount Carmel against the prophets of Baal, as seen in the story documented in 1 Kings 18–19. He, however, became depressed as fear gripped him as a result of a threat to his life that he "heard" was made by Jezebel. What he heard affected his soul as his emotions began to get the better of him. In this dread and fear, he fled and was hiding in an attempt to preserve his life. He was not able to consciously think that the same God who had brought him that major victory was able to preserve and keep him from the intended

The Battle of the Mind

threat of the enemy. He allowed fear to win the vote over faith because of his insecurity and seeming defeat. I surmised that he forgot that greater is He that was in him than he that was operating through and in Jezebel. He was focusing on what he heard and not seeing what God had just done in and through him.

Yes, this great hero had his share of the battle of the mind. His experience saw him receiving a personal visitation from God, right in the middle of his mental war, which had him retreating and in hiding. Irrespective of how anointed you are, the reality of life will come face to face with you. This is where your faith is put to the test; you are given the choice to make—lie over truth, faith over fear—right there in your time of despair and hopelessness.

Elijah was about to give up because of the spirit of depression that overtook him after a major battle and victory. God assured him that he was not alone in the struggle as many more had taken the same stand as he did and were susceptible to the same fate or threat (see 1 Kings 19:10,19). God's presence at that time was evidence that He was watching over him, and as such, He showed up to confirm this and console and instruct him concerning what was left undone that needed to be completed before exiting this life (see 1 Kings 19:15-17 and Psalm 118:17).

This encounter or visitation was intended to remind Elijah that even though he felt defeated, he was never defeated. The host of heaven's armies was with him. As such, he was told to rise, eat, and get renewed strength for the journey because this was not the end. It had only just begun.

We can also look at David as another point of reference. He is my hero and point of reference, and I pull strength from his many

The Battle of the Mind

encounters, his responses, and his testimonies of victory. Anointed and appointed but also faced discouragement and disappointment that made him fearful and engaged in the battle of the mind.

What was his response?

David said in Psalm 56:3–4, *"Whenever I am afraid, I will trust in You. In God (I will praise His word), In God I have put my trust; I will not fear. What can flesh do to me?" (NKJV).*

David understood that:

1. Lack and want were not his portion, as seen in Psalm 23:1.
2. Despite what he was facing, and would face, he would be restored, as seen in Psalm 23:2-3.
3. He was going through but would come out victorious, even when he came face to face with death, as seen in Psalm 23:4.
4. The table would be turned in his favour, and his enemies would be put to open shame, disgrace, and utter defeat, as seen in Psalm 23:5.
5. He was surrounded and protected by the angels called goodness and mercy, who were assigned to both sides of him: on the right and on the left. God was his ever-present help in times of trouble. When trouble was present, His God was never absent but right there in his circumstance, turning it around for his good.

What threat are you facing at this time? What are the lies the enemy is feeding your mind? Let the story of Elijah and the life of David be your points of reference, your ray of hope and source of strength and the motivation to resist and advance.

The Battle of the Mind

David, with a reset mind, declared in confidence and boasted in the source of his strength and victory in Psalm 18:28-50:

> *For You will light my lamp; the LORD my God will enlighten my darkness. For by You I can run against a troop, by my God I can leap over a wall. As for God, His way is perfect; The word of the LORD is proven; He is a shield to all who trust in Him. For who is God, except the LORD? And who is a rock, except our God? It is God who arms me with strength, and makes my way perfect. He makes my feet like the feet of deer, and sets me on my high places. He teaches my hands to make war, so that my arms can bend a bow of bronze. You have also given me the shield of Your salvation; Your right hand has held me up, Your gentleness has made me great. You enlarged my path under me, so my feet did not slip. I have pursued my enemies and overtaken them; Neither did I turn back again till they were destroyed. I have wounded them, so that they could not rise; They have fallen under my feet. For You have armed me with strength for the battle; You have subdued under me those who rose up against me. You have also given me the necks of my enemies, so that I destroyed those who hated me. They cried out, but there was none to save; Even to the LORD, but He did not answer them. Then I beat them as fine as the dust before the wind; I cast them out like dirt in the streets. You have delivered me from the strivings of the people; You have made me the head of the nations; A people I have not known shall serve me. As soon as they hear of me they obey me; The foreigners submit to me. The foreigners fade away, and come frightened from their hideouts. The LORD lives! Blessed be my Rock! Let the God of my salvation be exalted. It is God who avenges me, and subdues the peoples under*

> *me; He delivers me from my enemies. You also lift me up above those who rise against me; You have delivered me from the violent man. Therefore I will give thanks to You, O LORD, among the Gentiles, and sing praises to Your name. Great deliverance He gives to His king, and shows mercy to His anointed, to David and his descendants forevermore. (Psalm 18:24-50 – NKJV).*

The visitation or encounter that Elijah received in this dark hour of his life when he thought this was it and his assignment was complete was to reset his mindset and give him a few nuggets and snippets of what was left to be done.

I don't know the nature or intensity of the mental attack, but just know today that God has your back, and you are not alone in it; God is with you, backing you 100%.

The question was asked, *"What are you doing here, at this place of depression, alienation, and defeat?"* The same question is being asked of you, my friend. Elijah was challenged to reset his mind. He was reassured, comforted, and strengthened to be renewed and restored; today, likewise, you are too.

Like Elijah, you are being challenged to reset your mind to that of the *mindset of a warrior* and that *of Christ* because you are not alone.

You will not abort your purpose but will, with the help of God through a renewed mind, finish strong because the joy of the Lord is your strength.

The Battle of the Mind

> *So he answered and said to me: "This is the word of the LORD to Zerubbabel: 'Not by might nor by power, but by My Spirit,' Says the LORD of hosts. 'Who are you, O great mountain? Before Zerubbabel you shall become a plain! And he shall bring forth the capstone With shouts of "Grace, grace to it!"'" Moreover the word of the LORD came to me, saying: "The hands of Zerubbabel have laid the foundation of this temple; His hands shall also finish it. Then you will know that the LORD of hosts has sent Me to you. (Zechariah 4:6-9 – NKJV).*

> *Then he said to them, "Go your way, eat the fat, drink the sweet, and send portions to those for whom nothing is prepared; for this day is holy to our Lord. Do not sorrow, for the joy of the LORD is your strength." (Nehemiah 8:10 – NKJV).*

> *being confident of this very thing, that He who has begun a good work in you will complete it until the day of Jesus Christ; (Philippians 1:6 – NKJV).*

If the journey to recover and restore your mind seems to be taking time, be patient with yourself. It took years and months to have brought it to this point; hence, it will take time to renew the mind. It will be done over time and not overnight. Allow due process. The devil took time to sow those seeds, so it will take time to remove and destroy those weeds gradually.

When the mind has been out of alignment for some time, it takes time to reset; do not rush it. Be thorough in doing it. God did not complete creation in one day. Take it a day at a time, and you will eventually master it. It will happen gradually, not suddenly. God

The Battle of the Mind

has His ways or strategies of doing this perfectly. Just cooperate with Him as the Holy Spirit works alongside you as your Counselor or Helper to effect the change or transformation you so desire in order to be a victor in this battle.

> *I will not drive them out from before you in one year, lest the land become desolate and the beasts of the field become too numerous for you. Little by little I will drive them out from before you, until you have increased, and you inherit the land. And I will set your bounds from the Red Sea to the sea, Philistia, and from the desert to the River. For I will deliver the inhabitants of the land into your hand, and you shall drive them out before you. (Exodus 23:29-31 - NKJV).*

> *And the LORD your God will drive out those nations before you little by little; you will be unable to destroy them at once, lest the beasts of the field become too numerous for you. But the LORD your God will deliver them over to you, and will inflict defeat upon them until they are destroyed. (Deuteronomy 7:22-23 – NKJV).*

Do you have the mindset of a warrior who will not stop until the battle is completely won? We see that after David slew Goliath, he did not stop there; even though Goliath was now dead, David ensured that he removed his head. The head represents strength and glory, and as such, David removed it as evidence of total defeat of the enemy and, for Israel, absolute victory.

Let's look at another instance where another king was quite the opposite. Whilst David was intentional, King Joash was casual. Elijah instructed King Joash to strike the arrow of the Lord's deliverance, which would be a prophetic instruction requiring the

The Battle of the Mind

respective action to manifest God's deliverance from the oppression of the Assyrians. However, instead of constantly striking, King Joash was passive and casual about it, and as such, this was Elijah's response to him:

> *And Elisha said to him, "Take a bow and some arrows." So he took himself a bow and some arrows. Then he said to the king of Israel, "Put your hand on the bow." So he put his hand on it, and Elisha put his hands on the king's hands. And he said, "Open the east window"; and he opened it. Then Elisha said, "Shoot"; and he shot. And he said, "The arrow of the LORD's deliverance and the arrow of deliverance from Syria; for you must strike the Syrians at Aphek till you have destroyed them." Then he said, "Take the arrows"; so he took them. And he said to the king of Israel, "Strike the ground"; so he struck three times, and stopped. And the man of God was angry with him, and said, "You should have struck five or six times; then you would have struck Syria till you had destroyed it! But now you will strike Syria only three times." (2 Kings 13:15-19 - NKJV).*

God wants to deliver us mentally and emotionally more than we want to be delivered ourselves. How desperate are we for this freedom? We give up when we do not get instant results, and God has not given up on us and has delivered the enemy of our minds into our hands.

Keep striking the arrow of the Lord's deliverance concerning the battle of your mind until the mission to win it is totally accomplished. Do not stop striking by applying and declaring God's Word until you have totally broken free from the shackles over your mind.

The Battle of the Mind

Again, we see in Judges 20 where God gave the Israelites permission to go up against the Benjamites; however, they were beaten twice, but on the third attempt, according to God's instruction to them to go up against them, they succeeded and prevailed against them.

It is God's will for you to win the battle over your mind; as such, you must come into agreement with Him on this.

What are you thinking about? Be present where your thought pattern is concerned, and be conscious of what you are thinking. Be conscious enough to immediately identify when and where your mind is going off track and straying from the path of positivity.

Think about what you are thinking and how it is making you feel. If it causes discomfort, then, by all means, immediately do something to correct it. Cast down and displace the wrong thoughts with the right ones as guided by 2 Corinthians 10:4 and Philippians 4:8. Check carefully your thought patterns and evaluate and re-culture where necessary.

Release unhealthy thoughts from your mind and spirit because holding on to them will only keep you bound and oppressed, and eventually lead you into depression and distress because it is like an evil festering seed that, if left alone to linger, will establish roots or strongholds. If allowed to take hold, it will begin to take a toll on your body, eventually resulting in feelings of unrest, fatigue, stress, tension, and energy depletion. This, my friend, is definitely not in accordance with God's plan for your life.

Be determined and resolute to guard your mind and heart. What is flowing from your life and being experienced in your body is all

The Battle of the Mind

because of what is being fed, incubated, nurtured in your mind, and filtered into your spirit.

One way of identifying and alleviating what is happening is to identify or detect the trigger. What is the source or object that is negatively impacting your thought life and directing it in this negative path? What has caused these wonderings, ponderings, reasoning, and wanderings? Identify from when it all began.

The various occurrences in life can trigger happiness or sadness, depending on your response. This the devil knows, and as such, he monitors and uses each as an opportunity and to his advantage; he knows your strengths and weaknesses. He knows where and when to attack at your most vulnerable time. As such, you too must be vigilant and sober because the devil is an opportunist and a strategist. God, the Master Strategist, has given you the power over all the powers of the enemy. You must capitalize on this and always preempt the enemy. Be proactive and not reactive; you can outwit him, and that is how you will overcome him. Ambush and surprise him and destroy his plans and schemes concerning your mind because if he is successful in getting your mind, he is successful in getting your entire life.

Resetting the mind requires that we see whatever seems like a setback as a setup for a breakthrough or greater comeback. Greatness becomes a reality for those who do not allow failure to stop them from persisting in trying until they finally succeed.

The famous little gem I learned in kindergarten as I grew states: *"If at first you don't succeed, try again."* The origin of this phrase is not entirely clear, having been quoted as far back as 1840. Even from this developmental stage of life, we were being taught,

The Battle of the Mind

nurtured, and cultured to be persistent. As a child, we believed and embraced it and even embodied it. Still, as we grew and became—if I may say—more intelligent, intellectual, knowledgeable, and able to reason and rationalize, we threw away this confidence, belief, and resilience garnered. Instead, in response to challenges that see us failing, we give up or quit instead of going at it again.

We allow our minds to dictate and vote for us as it relates to our perception and perspective concerning the various situations we face. We totally forget who we are in God and what we have been taught accordingly. We need to access the power of resilience that is imputed in us to resist in the face of adversity. Confronting and conquering will definitely require resetting the mind and going back to our childish way of thinking. The childish way of thinking is that of the mind of Christ, as seen in Philippians 2:5 and Matthew 18:1-5, one of humility and confidence. Resetting the mind requires humility, as seen in Philippians 2:1-10. Humility is key to unlocking the way to victory.

Jesus Christ fell several times with the cross whilst carrying it, but He did not give up. He got back up again and kept going. He knew the world was depending on His persistence and obedience. The cause was greater than what He was currently experiencing. As such, His resurrection saw Him much stronger than He had been before. Likewise, true warriors who rise from failure are stronger than before the fall they experienced—they become wiser, braver, and more resilient.

We must always trust that all, even the worst, is working for the best, as seen in Romans 8:28.

The Battle of the Mind

Your mind is where it is at: the war/battle; be its commander, not its soldier. According to Ephesians 6:10-18, we must not just put on but keep on the entire armour, a part of which is the helmet that protects the head where the mind is located.

The process of resetting the mind entails focusing on what you can control and letting go of whatever you cannot. Rise with courage even when hope seems distant. Resetting is re-culturing to cultivate the warrior mindset.

To reset our minds from the dungeon of fear, we must climb. It takes courage to confront and conquer fear and leave it behind. It requires cultivating, attracting, and accommodating the right thoughts. This is dependent on the nature and object of your meditation, as seen in Psalm 1:2 (see also Joshua 1:8).

> *But his delight is in the law of the LORD, and in His law he meditates day and night. (Psalm 1:2 – NKJV).*

Reset your mind with God's Word and receive a new mindset. This will make you a force to reckon with against the forces of darkness, as seen in Ephesians 6:12. As such, you cannot be passive and naïve but spiritually aggressive and proactive (see Luke 10:19).

The enemy has no power over your mind unless you give that authority and permission to him.

"You have power over your mind – not outside events; realize this and you will find strength."

—Marcus Aurelius

The Battle of the Mind

In other words, it is not the circumstances, situations, or traumas that you may encounter that have the final say; it is your response of resilience and positivity towards it that makes that great difference.

Resetting your mind will require you to work your way back up after hitting rock bottom; this makes you unstoppable because you take no for an answer. You are not what happened to you. You do not have to become it if you choose to become the opposite. The outcome depends on your aspiration in accordance with the nature and present condition of your mind. Reset and refocus if you must, and you will see great or vast improvement and progress as you do. As you do, watch God keep you in His perfect peace as you keep and continue to keep your mind steadfastly stayed on Him, as seen in Isaiah 26:3.

The choice of a reset is yours to make; as such, make it wisely and swiftly before your mind is totally negatively captivated. It will take much time to retrieve and restore it. Save yourself the unnecessary efforts by beginning the combat to pursue, overtake, and recover all, as seen in 1 Samuel 13:8.

In a world filled with distractions, the ability to focus is a superpower, and as such, if one can master his attention, then by all means, with Christ, you will win at mastering your life because where your mind goes in that course or path, your life will flow.

As you seek to reset the mind, always choose wisdom over impulse or emotions. Be motivated to act or respond by revelation and not emotion. Feelings are fickle, and this is how the enemy seeks to trick us by playing on or targeting our emotions. Your mind is more powerful than the circumstances around us. We were given

The Battle of the Mind

dominion to conquer and reign and rule over all. You may not be able to control the events surrounding your life but you, through Jesus Christ, can always control your reaction or response to them.

In resetting the mind, peace will come from accepting what is and focusing on what can be; this is done by keeping your mind and focusing on God and what He says will be your reality or dream. Be assured that everything will seemingly get hard until it gets easy; it gets worse before it gets better. It comes apart before and because it is coming together.

We cannot learn without pain. There has to be pain because of the process; pressure has to be applied to extract whatever is precious and deeply hidden within. No pain, no purpose or gain; no fulfilment or full proof of your ministry.

When you reset your mind, you will see that success is not a matter of luck or bucking up but, rather, the result of hard work, perseverance, and a refusal to give up no matter the odds. You must be resolute that you will not be broken but made or created from what was intended to destroy you; you are becoming a lean, mean, fighting machine, as seen in Psalm 18:29-30 and Isaiah 41:15.

Never quit when you are tired; quit when you are done; you may withdraw to advance but never quit until you are done (see Philippians 1:6). As you go, persevere and turn every obstacle of the adversary in the adversities into opportunities.

Be in authority and control of your mind.

> *The centurion answered and said, "Lord, I am not worthy that You should come under my roof. But only speak a word,*

The Battle of the Mind

> *and my servant will be healed. For I also am a man under authority, having soldiers under me. And I say to this one, 'Go,' and he goes; and to another, 'Come,' and he comes; and to my servant, 'Do this,' and he does it." (Matthew 8:8-9 – NKJV).*

In this battle, may your heart beat with passion and purpose as you are engaged in the war for your mind. Be allergic to negativity but passionate about positivity. Cultivate a PMA always, even when the opposite presents itself. It takes a strong will to win this lifelong or age-old battle.

As you fight, you will discover your true self according to God's divine order. You see, the greatest and most important battle is internal. As you fight for the right to your mind, your heart must be filled with hope and determination to see transformation. Through discipline comes freedom; keep applying the truth as seen in John 8:32 & 36, 2 Timothy 1:7, and 1 John 4:18.

Your strength is built in silence and not in the applause of the crowd or noise. As you war this good warfare for your mind to experience this golden freedom, you must also come away from the crowd and go to the secret place in order to dominate when you emerge as a victor.

In resetting the mind, the following truth must be known: Godly wisdom helps us to win the war of the mind.

> *Hear, my children, the instruction of a father, and give attention to know understanding; Get wisdom! Get understanding! Do not forget, nor turn away from the words of my mouth. Do not forsake her, and she will preserve you;*

The Battle of the Mind

> *Love her, and she will keep you. Wisdom is the principal thing; Therefore get wisdom. And in all your getting, get understanding. (Proverbs 4:1, 5-7 – NKJV).*

The devil walks in wisdom because he is "wise in his own eyes." His wisdom is foolish and is destructive by his evil intent, as seen in John 10:10. We are admonished in Proverbs 3:7 *"**not** to be wise in your own eyes." (emphasis mine)*.

As such, we must walk in Godly wisdom so that we will not be entrapped by him and fall prey to or victim to his demise by way of his evil schemes and devices—all of which are launched or aimed at our minds.

Godly wisdom will help us guard and win the battle over our minds and not succumb to the arrows and darts of evil or wrong thoughts aimed at our minds daily.

It is with—or by—Godly wisdom that we will be trained and empowered to ward off and cast down every thought that presents itself that is not of God to its destruction.

With Godly wisdom, you will not walk the paths that your wrong thoughts want to take you. With Godly wisdom, you will be able to stay the course of right and Godly thinking. The war must first be won in the mind in order for all else in your life to be divinely aligned.

Godly wisdom is valuable; do not underestimate it. It is a powerful weapon of mass destruction against the enemy's plan to win and gain control of your mind.

The Battle of the Mind

With Godly wisdom, we can be proactive as we discern and preempt the enemy's plan and schemes by first identifying the mental seed he is trying to sow in the womb of our minds.

The battle begins and ends in the mind; we must possess Godly wisdom by all means if we are to win. As such, if we acknowledge that we lack it, ask for it because this is how we will be properly equipped to win the battle of the mind.

Also, in order to win his battle, we must know that Jesus Christ died for the victory of the mind. Just as there is a battle for it, there is a victory for it that has already been won and sealed. The price is fully paid on the cross of Calvary, and a sealed deal is made by way of an empty grave.

John 19:30 and Matthew 28:6 speak to the finished work of Jesus Christ and a fight already fixed in our favour. Yes, it is a certainty that Jesus Christ died for the victory over your mind. When He said, "It is finished," He meant that when the battle to regain victory over your mind ensued, you would engage the enemy in this war to win and re-claim it because it has already been finished.

Do not be naive and passive concerning the ensuing battle, which has been from the beginning. Instead, be vigilant and sober because the enemy will not give in to his already fate of defeat.

Until time turns to eternity, we must keep fighting this battle from the point of victory, knowing that Jesus Christ has already won it on the cross and, because He wears the victor's crown, all we must do is claim it and wear it. Jesus won it so that we can win it. How do we do this? Philippians 2:5 says we adopt the mind of Christ; yes, let this mind be in you. As you put on the whole armour of God

The Battle of the Mind

as guided in Ephesians 6:10-18, wear the helmet of salvation as seen in John 3:16-17 and receive God's full and free salvation, which includes healing, deliverance and liberation; this is His guaranteed protection. Your head was designed to wear the victor's crown, just as Jesus did.

Jesus Christ came, died, rose again, and ascended to give us total and permanent liberation, as seen in John 8:32, 36. Your victory and liberty totally depend on you standing on the truth of God concerning you, being fully persuaded by it, and walking by faith in it.

CHAPTER 3

THE MINDSET OF A WARRIOR

With the mindset of a warrior, you always see a comeback and a greater one after a setback. This is the mind that the worshipping warrior, David, had. He would not take no for an answer or defeat as final. We see this quite evident in the following passages in 1 Samuel 16 as he confronted Goliath. He did not see from his natural eyes or hear from his natural ears, as seen in Isaiah 11:2-3 and in 1 Samuel 30 when defeat was staring him straight in the face. He always sees the "all things working together and coming together for good." He understood that it had to come apart in order to come together for the better part of the story: for God's glory.

> *Then he took his staff in his hand; and he chose for himself five smooth stones from the brook, and put them in a shepherd's bag, in a pouch which he had, and his sling was in his hand. And he drew near to the Philistine. So the Philistine came, and began drawing near to David, and the man who bore the shield went before him. And when the Philistine looked about and saw David, he disdained him; for he was only a youth, ruddy and good-looking. So the Philistine said to David, "Am I a dog, that you come to me with sticks?" And the Philistine cursed David by his*

gods. And the Philistine said to David, "Come to me, and I will give your flesh to the birds of the air and the beasts of the field!" Then David said to the Philistine, "You come to me with a sword, with a spear, and with a javelin. But I come to you in the name of the LORD of hosts, the God of the armies of Israel, whom you have defied. This day the LORD will deliver you into my hand, and I will strike you and take your head from you. And this day I will give the carcasses of the camp of the Philistines to the birds of the air and the wild beasts of the earth, that all the earth may know that there is a God in Israel. Then all this assembly shall know that the LORD does not save with sword and spear; for the battle is the LORD's, and He will give you into our hands." So it was, when the Philistine arose and came and drew near to meet David, that David hurried and ran toward the army to meet the Philistine. Then David put his hand in his bag and took out a stone; and he slung it and struck the Philistine in his forehead, so that the stone sank into his forehead, and he fell on his face to the earth. So David prevailed over the Philistine with a sling and a stone, and struck the Philistine and killed him. But there was no sword in the hand of David. Therefore David ran and stood over the Philistine, took his sword and drew it out of its sheath and killed him, and cut off his head with it. And when the Philistines saw that their champion was dead, they fled. (1 Samuel 17:40-51 – NKJV).

Now it happened, when David and his men came to Ziklag, on the third day, that the Amalekites had invaded the South and Ziklag, attacked Ziklag and burned it with fire, and had taken captive the women and those who were there, from small to great; they did not kill anyone, but carried them

The Battle of the Mind

away and went their way. So David and his men came to the city, and there it was, burned with fire; and their wives, their sons, and their daughters had been taken captive. Then David and the people who were with him lifted up their voices and wept, until they had no more power to weep. And David's two wives, Ahinoam the Jezreelitess, and Abigail the widow of Nabal the Carmelite, had been taken captive. Now David was greatly distressed, for the people spoke of stoning him, because the soul of all the people was grieved, every man for his sons and his daughters. But David strengthened himself in the LORD his God. Then David said to Abiathar the priest, Ahimelech's son, "Please bring the ephod here to me." And Abiathar brought the ephod to David. So David inquired of the LORD, saying, "Shall I pursue this troop? Shall I overtake them?" And He answered him, "Pursue, for you shall surely overtake them and without fail recover all." So David went, he and the six hundred men who were with him, and came to the Brook Besor, where those stayed who were left behind. But David pursued, he and four hundred men; for two hundred stayed behind, who were so weary that they could not cross the Brook Besor. (1 Samuel 30:1-10 – NKJV).

Then David attacked them from twilight until the evening of the next day. Not a man of them escaped, except four hundred young men who rode on camels and fled. So David recovered all that the Amalekites had carried away, and David rescued his two wives. And nothing of theirs was lacking, either small or great, sons or daughters, spoil or anything which they had taken from them; David recovered all. Then David took all the flocks and herds they had driven

The Battle of the Mind

> *before those other livestock, and said, "This is David's spoil." (1 Samuel 30:17–20 – NKJV).*

Again, we see David resetting his mind after a seeming defeat to which he was not about to concede. With a reset mind, he decided to consult God regarding how to approach this humiliating situation. Certainly, he was given a favourable response because he had the mindset of a warrior.

The mindset of the warrior is not given but cultivated during battle. This is how mental strength, stamina, and agility are cultivated, built, and maintained. To win the battle of the mind, you must cultivate and maintain a warrior's mindset. To overcome and be in control of the mind, you must have a warrior mentality or the mindset of a warrior—one where you are resolute to defend your territory from the mental intruder. Your mind is your God-given inheritance or property, and as such, it should not be under any other influence than that of God Almighty.

As warriors, it is the battle that mantles us. Stripes are earned because of the wounds received, nurtured, and healed. As such, we cannot allude to concede but to resist and fight to maintain and regain the territory of our mind that was given to us by God.

If there is no battle, how can you celebrate victory? If there is no victory in your battle, where is the credibility of your story of God's goodness and glory? What is the validity of your testimony? You cannot roll over and surrender your mind to the enemy because if you do, you are actually surrendering your entire life to him.

We must rule or control our minds, or it will rule or control us. The alpha in us will only rise when we begin to take control of our minds in accordance with God's strategy and design—keeping it in alignment with His will according to the object and subject of meditation.

The warrior's mindset requires that you never quit despite how hard the fight gets. Strength comes as you push and endure to the end. Keep declaring and believing that you can and will do all things through Christ who strengthens you, as seen in Philippians 4:13.

True bravery is the act of facing our fears and acting accordingly despite the presence of them. Believe it or not, the greatest battle we will ever face is in and always originates in our minds.
You fight back by never allowing life's punches to break you but build you. Use the lemons given to you to make lemonade, as the common saying goes. Put on your gloves and stay in the ring to win.

As a warrior, according to God's Word, you stand for what you believe in. Keep declaring until you begin to experience the victory. Whatever is fighting you, fight it, do not accept it, do not fear it, take control, and force it to lose its hold.

Fight for what is right, even when it is not popular. Choose to maintain the right mindset. It is never popular to think right, and as such, this makes the challenge great, but with great faith, you will prevail. Do not watch the crowd or majority or because everybody is thinking it. You and God are a majority.

Great heights are reached by walking rough paths, so when you have reached this path on your journey to destiny, do not turn back or quit and sit; keep going. Cultivate and maintain the mind to keep going despite the challenges. This is the warrior mindset.

The Battle of the Mind

To cultivate and maintain the mindset of a warrior, you must understand that the path to success is paved with stones called challenges, and underneath them are valuable lessons. With the mindset of a warrior, you can see beyond the stones called challenges, focus on learning the lessons, and pass your tests with flying colours. Fight to rise above your limitations because they are already under your feet.

What is amazing about a warrior is that the warrior's heart doesn't only fight for the freedom of himself but also for others. They also know without even the shadow of the presence of doubt that you never lose, but either you win or learn; either way, it is victory anyway and anyhow.

Our greatest enemy is never found on the outside but from within. To win the battle, you have to sweat more in training so you will bleed less in the war. Prepare for combat by not being ignorant of the enemy's devices and strategies against the mind. Be proactive in guarding it with the implantation and embodying of the Word of God. Be in attack-mode by your declaration of God's Word, not in defense or retreat. Be the predator and not the prey; be in pursuit and not being pursued.

A warrior fights, not just with his mind, but also with his spirit. Both entities must be in agreement. The mind, most times, opposes the spirit, as seen in Galatians 5:17 and Romans 8:5-8:

> *For the flesh lusts against the Spirit, and the Spirit against the flesh; and these are contrary to one another, so that you do not do the things that you wish. (Galatians 5:17 – NKJV).*

The Battle of the Mind

> *For those who live according to the flesh set their minds on the things of the flesh, but those who live according to the Spirit, the things of the Spirit. For to be carnally minded is death, but to be spiritually minded is life and peace. Because the carnal mind is enmity against God; for it is not subject to the law of God, nor indeed can be. So then, those who are in the flesh cannot please God. (Romans 8:5-8 - NKJV).*

A true warrior understands that he/she never loses and, as such, learns from every setback and emerges stronger with a greater comeback. Practice like you have never won and perform like you have never lost but have only learnt, even from past and present mistakes. Your success is not realized in your attempt to avoid failure but in learning from it and becoming a better or best version of you because of it. Always remember that better never settles until it becomes the best.

A warrior's bravery shines brightest when the night is darkest. When your situation is at its worst, and you decide not to reverse or retreat but to advance in the face of diverse adversity, that is when your strength is definitely evident.

Building the warrior in you as you battle the war of the mind requires that you seek out challenges, as they are the melting pots in which your character is refined and redefined. Every trial you may face or have faced is intended to build the foundation of who you will become according to God's blueprint for your life—refining and defining the God-given character required in you.

The spirit of a warrior is unconquerable and undefeatable. He/she fights not for fame but for the greater good. As such, he must be

The Battle of the Mind

loyal and honourable and totally committed to his assignment despite the attacks that are being waged in his mind.

The path of progress will never be easy; as such, on the easy path, you won't progress but instead regress. The mindset of a warrior requires that you set your face like a flint so you do not flinch or wink in fear.

A warrior does not bow to defeat but rises stronger than before. As such, a warrior must embrace challenges as opportunities to grow.

As I faced the reality of the most recent attack, as I earlier shared, which led me to write this book, I then understood that if I am to be out of the woods, I will have to acknowledge that this life is a battle, and to survive the attacks is the way to comeback. As such, I will have to cultivate the mindset of a warrior because, daily, there is a conquest. I understood that you cannot be casual or laid back or think that, oh, I might as well just lay back or roll over and die. This is not the life that God designed for me. According to God's standards, my life is to be lived by design and not by crisis. I also acknowledged that many of the crisis we face are self-inflicted or created because of our mental deficiency and our will that we have surrendered to the enemy. We are pretty much guilty of throwing ourselves into the pit of hungry lions who are waiting to devour our God-given destiny. For every mistake, God has made a way of escape as a result of his great lovingkindness, faithfulness, and tender mercies, as seen in 1 Corinthians 10:13.

> *No temptation has overtaken you except such as is common to man; but God is faithful, who will not allow you to be tempted beyond what you are able, but with the temptation*

> *will also make the way of escape, that you may be able to bear it. (1 Corinthians 10:13 – NKJV).*

If you got in, there is a way out; cultivate the warrior mindset and fight your way out to freedom.

Never be ashamed of your scars because they are your symbols or trophies of your survival. True warriors fight for the love that fills their hearts, even in the face of impossible odds. A warrior's heart is a source of inspiration or a point of reference to many others.

Never lose hope in hard times, but get harder and stronger in that crucible of fire. The only limits that exist are those you believe. There is nothing impossible to him who trusts God and believes for that which you have conceived. You can and will give birth to it.

Learn from every battle fought. Take control of your future by mastering your present. Never be anxious about the future; just see and embrace it as you await it in faith. Anxiety is one of the enemy's dangerous and deadly weapons; do not take it lightly. Anxiety comes because of uncertainty and insecurity. It is rooted in the fear of the unknown. Trust the future into God's hands and let Him take full control. This is one of the many ways you resist and fight.

Your body can withstand almost anything; as such, it is your mind that you have to convince that, through Christ, you can do all things. True strength comes from within and is established in the womb of the mind. A great warrior is disciplined and persevering, as seen in 2 Timothy 1:7 and Philippians 4:13.

As a warrior, you must possess a strong but loving, gentle, compassionate heart filled with courage. Challenges are not stop

The Battle of the Mind

signs but guidelines for growth. See challenges you are faced with as a stepping stone to go further, higher and deeper, to get stronger and wiser. As a warrior, your legacy should be written in your deed, not your words, because action speaks louder than words.

A warrior is made from the various battles he or she has fought, knowing and embracing the concept according to the truth in God's Word that you were born to win, and as such, you live to conquer. Fight with honour and fairly, even when no one is watching.

As an unknown philosopher quoted, *"A gem cannot be polished without friction, nor a man perfected without trials."* Hence, there is a need to cultivate and maintain the mindset of a warrior in order to win this lifelong battle that began in the Garden of Eden.

"The nearer a man comes to a calm mind, the closer he is to strength."

—*Marcus Aurelius*

Assuredly, your meekness is not your weakness but your strength under control.

The heart of a warrior beats with purpose, signaling that survival is a must. There is a worthy cause for which this battle is being ensued and fought; as such, there is no room for retreating, surrendering, or quitting. For the warrior, every challenge is a learning experience, as your situation is your teacher and examiner. The challenges are assessments aimed at evaluating your current state, and where you have failed; you will be required to be retrained until you have graduated and elevated to another level or rank.

The Battle of the Mind

Overcoming your fears by facing them is what is required of a true warrior. Whatever you fear doing most, know that that is what you need to be pursuing.

The testament to the power of resilience lies within the spirit of a true warrior. It is his testament or credible evidence of a positive change in the way of seeing, thinking, and doing things. Waging good warfare also includes staying humble and letting your actions speak volumes. Do not allow your mind to tell you otherwise.

A warrior stands even in the face of adversity and does not divert to hopelessness or despondency. He/she is motivated and fueled by faith. Control your mind, and you will control your destiny; this is the mindset of a true warrior who knows the importance of the mind or his mental womb, which controls his life and destiny.

Your passion for true, long, and lasting freedom will push or propel you like Hannah, a woman of persistence. The moment you choose persistence, challenges become teachers and not a threat. You can either turn trials into triumph or defeat and obstacles into fuel or excuses. The choice is yours; which will it be? How do you overcome challenges? Begin to see them as a part of the journey. Do not be startled by them but expect and ask for grace to deal with them individually with wisdom, tenacity, and the expectation of ultimate victory with every experience. This will make you a point of reference and influence: a bonafide warrior.

Change the mindset to that of a warrior, and you will definitely change the challenge as you will always see it in your favour. Unlike the Israelite spies, you will not see yourself as the grasshopper but the giant, not the victim but the victor, not the loser but the winner. If you desire victory in this battle of the mind, this

The Battle of the Mind

is not a maybe but a must. The true warrior must have insight and hindsight, where judgment is not done from the natural eyes.

A gentle reminder is that there are some battles we may be required to have support, but there are others that require us to be or walk it or fight it alone; however, this lonely path is designed to be an inspiration to many who will need it as a point of reference in their time of need, as they too will be required to trod this lonely path of theirs being ensued in the battle of the mind.

The Word of God says in Matthew 11:12, and I paraphrase, that from ancient times, the representatives of the kingdom are forcefully and violently opposed and, as such, cannot and should not respond to the threat of war or battle any less or casually or passively but forcefully and aggressively. It is generally said that the causal and passive become casualties of war. Therefore, when you meet a swordsman, you draw your sword and do not recite poetry to one who is not a poet. The fight must be even or commensurate. Never roll over and die because of passiveness, being naïve and casual. You must have the mindset of a warrior where you take no threat for granted, especially that against your mind, which is the engine of your life.

For a warrior or a faith-walker and a truth talker, failure is not final, neither is delay a denial; neither does conquest say that it is over.

> *And the Lord visited Sarah as He had said, and the Lord did for Sarah as He had spoken. For Sarah conceived and bore Abraham a son in his old age, at the set time of which God had spoken to him. And Abraham called the name of his son who was born to him—whom Sarah bore to him—Isaac. (Genesis 21:1-3 – NKJV).*

The Battle of the Mind

When Jehovah has the final say, failure is not final because nothing works against us, but all things work together for our good because of your love and devotion to God and His purpose for our lives. He ultimately gets the glory from our trials and failures and ultimate success.

Failure is not final. You do not have to forfeit or abort your prophetic destiny because of past or present mistakes that you have made.

Abraham erred, but in his weakness, he did not dwell there but continued forward in faith. In other words, he dug another well when that well was blocked up with doubt. In some of his instances of failure, he even uttered his fears from his mouth (see Genesis 12:10-13, Genesis 20:2). He did not dwell in guilt and self-condemnation. He was guided by Romans 8:1.

> *There is therefore now no condemnation to those who are in Christ Jesus, who do not walk according to the flesh, but according to the Spirit. (Romans 8:1 – NKJV).*

Abraham feared what would have happened to him as he entered Egypt and Gerar, and as such, he lied. He feared Sarah's rejection and feeling of disappointment if he had rejected her suggestion, and as such, he succumbed to the fear of her pressure.

He however acknowledged that this would only be his final destination if he permitted it to be. He understood that he had the course of his life in his own hands and that the outcome depended on his reaction to the situation at hand. He made the wrong decision and action—one that was deceptive, faithless, and unnecessary. He allowed his emotions to vote and win over the revelation he had

The Battle of the Mind

received from God. However, from this setback he overcame and had a mighty comeback. From the mistakes made came lessons which he used to solidify his faith, which we see was again put to the test in Genesis 22.

We see along the journey to destiny where Abraham was put to several tests to try the strength of his faith, which he failed:

— In Egypt (see Genesis 12:10-13)
— In Gerar (see Genesis 20:1-2)
— Approached by Sarah (see Genesis 16:1-4)

Yes, Abraham flunked them all, but for God, failure is not final. We see this truth also evident in the story of Peter in his act of denial (see Matthew 26:69-75, John 21:1-17). We see this truth also evident in Genesis 21:1-7, where Isaac was eventually born to Abraham and Sarah according to God's plan.

From Abraham's mistakes came lessons that established mountain-like faith. We, like Abraham, can use our mistakes to establish mountain-like faith. We can also learn from the mistakes he had made. It is evident that he too experienced this battle of the mind.

Failure is not final because God always has the final call or say. He is right there in the midst of it all, going through with you. Failure is not final because there is a comeback from your setback. Your latter is greater than your past, and your best days are ahead and not behind. He still has you on His radar or on His mind, as seen in Jeremiah 29:11 and Proverbs 19:21.

God has a bigger and better plan than you can even think or imagine.

The Battle of the Mind

> *Now to Him who is able to do exceedingly abundantly above all that we ask or think, according to the power that works in us. (Ephesians 3:20 – NKJV).*

Do not be defined by the mistakes you have made. Shake off the dust of guilt and self-condemnation, get back up again, and keep moving in faith, focusing forward and running this race.

You are not the mistakes you made; do not let them define you. Let God's Word define and realign you because it says you are a success because there is no failure in Him. According to 2 Corinthians 5:17, being in Christ makes one a new creature; old things or mistakes are in the past, put under the blood, and nailed to the cross. As such, it is time to get up and move forward into the new and receive the fresh dew of heaven.

Arise from the past, focus, and be present in your present as you aspire towards the future. Focus on going across to access, conquer, and possess.

The mindset of a warrior requires focus and great courage. Yes, it takes great boldness, as seen in Proverbs 28:1.

Distraction redirects your gaze from that which is positive and most important. It shifts your priority and meditation from that which is positively of most importance to that of insignificance (see Matthew 6:33, Colossians 3:2). It is shifting one's attention from the God-given mission, assignment or vision to one's self—its desire and self-preservation. The distraction is intended to derail you.

The Battle of the Mind

To cultivate this warrior mindset, you must fix your focus right, and where there is a shift, reset or realign accordingly, immediately.

Focus on the future glory and not the present suffering according to your story. This process that seems like eternity is, in God's eye, just temporary (see Hebrews 12:2, 2 Corinthians 4:7, 1 Peter 1:6, 1 Peter 4:13, and Romans 8:17).

Check your meditation because what you magnify, you give life.

Even the smallest of confidence in God goes a long way if, as a warrior, you are to remain in the fight and emerge the victor. This confidence is the source from which you gain the courage to not give up in life, not even over the battle of your mind. Even when it seems as if the fight is going nowhere, take courage; the fight is fixed in your favour. You just have to cooperate by girding up the loins of your mind with God's Truth.

I want to reiterate and emphasize that we cannot underestimate what is going on in our minds. Real spiritual war is waged by the enemy in our minds and we must train our minds to fight. If our mind is worth having, it is worth fighting for.

We must train our minds to fight, resist, and not quit. Never succumb to the pressure of the adversary. Train your mind to run through troops and leap over walls; it is called the mindset of a warrior.

Do not follow your mind, but let it follow you. You have been given dominion and authority over it; do not allow it to make you trip. Be your mind's leader and not its follower. God has given you power over your mind, as seen in Romans 12:2 and Luke 10:19.

The Battle of the Mind

Fight back by submitting to God and resisting the devil and he will flee. This is how you move from being pursued to being in pursuit and accessing the victory. It is time to take it back. Like Ziklag, the enemy has launched an attack, but we cannot roll over and die. There is a warrior on the inside; let him arise. It is time to soar and climb to new heights. Break the threshold of staying in his stronghold as a victim and with a victim mindset.

If you have fallen, like any mighty warrior, get back up and go again; the brave, though he may fall, never yields, as seen in Proverbs 24:16. Like David, find the strength, encourage yourself in God, and enquire of Him as seen 1 Samuel 30:6-8. Fight to win because you can do all things through Christ's strength and grace. You are already fighting a battle that Jesus Christ has already won on your behalf (see 1 Corinthians 15:54-58). You must remain steadfast and unmovable in your mind.

When fear comes, do not go into flight mode but, instead, go into fight mode. Be mantled for the battle. Your battles are platforms set for your performance; as such, you should be mantled for them.

Cultivate the right mindset to be mantled for the battle because battles are the lifestyle or reality of a warrior. If we do not have the right mentality, we will not be able to survive, let alone win it. Consistency is an attribute of the enemy, and we must also be consistent if we are to win this battle of the mind. Based on the territories we have to conquer, we must be mantled for the battle.

God has made you a lean, fighting machine, as seen in Isaiah 41:8-16:

The Battle of the Mind

> *For I, the LORD your God, will hold your right hand, Saying to you, 'Fear not, I will help you.' "Fear not, you worm Jacob, You men of Israel! I will help you," says the LORD and your Redeemer, the Holy One of Israel. "Behold, I will make you into a new threshing sledge with sharp teeth; You shall thresh the mountains and beat them small, and make the hills like chaff. You shall winnow them, the wind shall carry them away, and the whirlwind shall scatter them; You shall rejoice in the LORD, and glory in the Holy One of Israel. (Isaiah 41:13-16 – NKJV).*

If you faint in the days of adversity, where is your strength? If you are wearied and intimidated by the footmen, what will happen when confronted by the horsemen?

> *If you faint in the day of adversity, your strength is small. (Proverbs 24:10 – NKJV).*

> *"If you have run with the footmen, and they have wearied you, then how can you contend with horses? And if in the land of peace, in which you trusted, they wearied you, Then how will you do in the floodplain of the Jordan?" (Jeremiah 12:5 – NKJV).*

Do not retreat in defeat. Train your mind to fight. Be mantled for the battle.

Reset your mind because it matters, and if you do not, it will hurt. Be re-cultured and mantled, begin to operate, and respond with a warrior mindset in order to win the battle consistently and constantly. Walk in freedom as a result of the victory.

The Prayer of Deliverance and Freedom

Lord, I thank You that my head is anointed and my cup overflows. I thank You that Your goodness and mercy follow me all the days of my life as I dwell in Your presence. I thank You for leading me beside still waters to restore my mind and heal my soul for Your name's sake and for Your glory. I thank You that Your sovereign Spirit is upon me, and as such, by You, I run through troops and leap over walls. I thank You that truly I am filled with power and might because Your Spirit and the fear of God is upon my life; as such, I am filled with wisdom, understanding, knowledge, counsel, and might.

I declare and decree that I am focused and will not be derailed by wrong thoughts, in the mighty name of Jesus. I gird up my loins with Your truth, and as such, I am being made totally free, in the mighty name of Jesus. I thank You that as I bring every thought captive to the obedience of Christ, that I am gaining victory over every mind-binding and every mind-controlling spirit assigned to derail me through wrong thinking. I put on the full armour of Your Word, including the helmet of salvation. I declare that I have the mind of Christ, and as such, there is no guilt or condemnation because I am of God. I am an overcomer and more than a conqueror because I am being transformed by the renewing of my mind to prove Your perfect will for my life.

The Battle of the Mind

I thank You that, because of the revelation and application of Your truth to my life, I have been set and made free from being held captive mentally, emotionally, and spiritually. Thank You for keeping me in perfect peace as I keep my mind stayed on You.

I declare and decree that, as of now, anxiety, worry, insecurity, fear, doubt, depression, hopelessness, rejection, discouragement, and disappointment are not my portion because I am perfected in Your love, joy, and peace. I have the mind of Christ and am made perfect in Your love.

I repent of wrong thoughts and actions that attracted those negative meditations and manifestations. As I renounce them, in the mighty name of Jesus Christ, I command every spirit attached to them to leave my life, never to return.

I choose, as of now, right and Godly thoughts based on the Word of God and remain forever the victor in and through Christ over the circumstances that I will face in my life. I choose to walk and live by faith and life by design with my mind and not by crisis and challenges that I may be experiencing or will ever experience.

I thank You that for this victory You died for, and by Your grace, I am appropriating it, in the name of Jesus Christ, the Liberator of my mind, spirit, soul, and body. I thank You that, as of today and thereafter, I receive Your truth and complete freedom for which Christ died, as I apply Your blood to my mind and life, in the name of Jesus Christ. For this, I give You thanks. In Jesus' name. Amen and Amen.

MY NOTES

THE JOURNEY TO DESTINY SERIES

Copies are available on Amazon both in Kindle and paperback

Other Purchasing Option:

Email (*For paperback only*): <u>Dailymannadevotionals@gmail.com</u>

ASPIRING TO INSPIRE

My heart is overflowing with a good theme; I recite my composition concerning the King; my tongue is the pen of a ready writer. (Psalm 45:1 – NKJV).

The Lord GOD has given me the tongue of the learned, that I should know how to speak a word in season to him who is weary. He awakens me morning by morning, He awakens my ear to hear as the learned. (Isaiah 50:4 – NKJV).

BLB My Quotes:

"Being productive in my place of affliction: my pain producing purpose. As a result, you are reading because I was bleeding, and I choose to make my meditation be my medication."

BLB My Quotes:

"Like an oyster hidden in the pearl of great price for which you have to dig deep in order to seek; so is your purpose hidden in your pain and is revealed at a great price called sacrifice, so that your story can become God's glory."

The Battle of the Mind – The Journey to Freedom and Victory, *as* divinely inspired by the Holy Spirit, was written by the author, Brendalee Bonnie of St. Catherine, Jamaica.

This book was revealed to me during one of those low times of my life when there was another visit by the spirit of fear. As I grappled with the current situation on hand, which got so overwhelming, I felt as if I was actually mentally drowning by the floodwaters of negative thoughts that were bombarding my mind. I felt as if I was about to succumb when I received a call that opened my eyes to the reality of my circumstance, which was more spiritual than natural. After coming to my senses and realizing what I was facing and how I must approach it if I was to survive and thrive, I was led to write this book based on the answer I sensed in my spirit: overcoming by cultivating the mindset of a warrior because as long as there is life, the battle of the mind will be an ongoing one.

As I am challenged, strengthened, encouraged, and comforted accordingly, I aspire to inspire others who are seeking an answer and seeking strength and direction to go along the Journey to Destiny.

Finding and knowing the truth is the only way to be truly made free; this truth is found in God's Word, which I am inspired to write.

I thank the God of heaven for using me to be a ready writer to give a word to those who need it as they seek. I understand what it is like being on the receiving end because when His Spirit speaks to me, He relieves my troubled mind. His Voice indeed makes the biggest difference one can ever find. He speaks all the time, but the deep secrets are revealed in the secret place as you set quality quiet time to seek His face and wait as you receive His grace.

This book aims to help the reader understand the reality of the spiritual and the potential danger of cultivating wrong thoughts. Also, it is important to identify and address them immediately. Being proactive in this mental battle is the best approach. It reduces the need to be reactive; in other words, prevention is better than cure. The only plan of action and reality to embrace, and the only way to be the victor is by changing your approach and cultivating a warrior's mindset in order to remain in the game of life. Also, be mindful of the truth that just as the mind is the place of the enemy's attack, it is the womb where God intends to give birth to that which He intends according to His thoughts and plan towards you.

THE JOURNEY TO DESTINY
SERIES

Brendalee Bonnie was born in the parish of St. Catherine. She gave her life to the Lord at the tender age of sixteen. Her passion is singing and living for God. Later in her life, with a new mandate and call of God on her life, she realized that she has a passion to inspire people, not just from a spiritual level, but in every other aspect of life.

Brendalee's passion for God and for helping others motivated her to successfully complete the level one counseling course at WAFIF Christian College (WCC). This accomplishment was ordained by God because it allowed her to get the proper training needed to professionally and effectively develop a God-given gift nestled within her.

As the Bible states in 2 Timothy 3:15-17, it is important to be equipped and thoroughly furnished for every good work. This course also confirmed the assignment as a helper/encourager, thereby confirming the prompting and passion to share in order to heal and empower others by giving strength to the weak, inspiration to the weary, and salvation to the lost.

With the heart of a servant, her tongue has been made the pen of a ready writer, one of the learned. The message of encouragement and empowerment is thereby communicated through her writing, giving a word in season to those who need it.

As commissioned in Luke 4:18-19 and Isaiah 61:1-2, Brendalee has answered the call to help heal the brokenhearted and help them to experience true freedom through her life-changing spiritual encounter as it is shared in this book. The objective is to help as she has been helped and to help deliver and liberate as she has been delivered and liberated as the truth is revealed. Her desire is to be able to identify with others in their struggle in the respective areas that she has struggled in and be able to help them get out as she, through the help of God, got out.

In her professional career, Brendalee works as an Administrative Assistant. She thoroughly enjoys her job, the highest point of which involves interacting with people at all levels. Each challenge encourages and pushes her to improve her personality, perception of others, and people skills. Her strengths are being passionate about God and helping, encouraging, comforting, and caring for the needs of others.

www.ingramcontent.com/pod-product-compliance
Lightning Source LLC
Chambersburg PA
CBHW050705160426
43194CB00010B/2003